MY Love STORY!!

3

Story KAZUNE KAWAHARA
Art ARUKO

MY love STORY!!

STORY Thus Far...

Takeo Goda, a first-year high school student, is a hot-blooded guy who is 6'6" tall and weighs 265 pounds. Boys look up to him, but the girls he falls in love with all end up liking his handsome best friend, Sunakawa!

Takeo gets his first girlfriend after he saves a girl named Yamato from a molester! Yamato's friends decide to have a mixer, but at the event, a fire breaks out! Takeo risks his life to save two of Yamato's friends who were unable to get away in time. Later, older students from the judo team beg Takeo to enter a tournament, which he wins magnificently! Yamato swoons over his performance! ♡

For Yamato's birthday, Takeo tries to please her with a plan he made with Sunakawa's help. When he learns that her birthday is the same as the day that Sunakawa's father is having surgery, however, he interrupts their date to be by Sunakawa's side. The surgery is a success, and when Yamato catches up to them, she is moved to tears by Takeo's kindness. Sunakawa comments on how nice it is to see Takeo and Yamato together...

MY
Love
STORY!!

HI, THIS IS ARUKO!

Whenever I draw Takeo, all I can think about is how cool he is.

Volume 3 is out! Thank you for all your support. ♡

In 2012, I came to truly realize how many people love Takeo. And the more I draw Yamato and Sunakawa, the more I love them! I'm so happy and thrilled and having so much fun! And I'm drawing as well as I can, so please keep reading!

I hope to see you in Volume 4 too. —— ♡

2013.2

I LOVE YOU...

LOOK, TAKEO!

DANDELIONS...

...AND WHITE CLOVERS!

YAMATO...

YOU LOOK LIKE A PRINCE!

I LOVE YOU.

YAMATO...

mountain

NOTHING'S GOING TO TEAR ME AWAY FROM YOUR SIDE TODAY.

AWW, C'MON! THERE'S NOTHING TO WORRY ABOUT!

MY BIRTHDAY WAS AMAZING, REMEMBER? BUT THIS MAKES ME REALLY HAPPY TOO. ♥

YAMATO AND I DECIDED TO RE-CELEBRATE HER BIRTHDAY BY GOING ON A PICNIC.
AH HA HA HA
HEH HEH HEH
HEY...
YOUR BAG LOOKS HEAVY. LET ME CARRY IT.
HEFT
WHAT'VE YOU GOT IN HERE?
UM... MOSTLY FOOD AND DRINKS AND STUFF.
PLUS TOWELS, A PICNIC BLANKET, TRASH BAGS...
TA-DA!
THIS IS ALL FOOD ?!
IT MUST'VE BEEN HARD FOR HER TO CARRY ALL THIS!
DID I MAKE TOO MUCH? I MIGHT'VE GONE OVERBOARD.
WILL YOU BE ABLE TO EAT IT ALL?
DING

THAT'S GOOD!
YAMATO...
THAT BROOCH LOOKS GREAT ON YOU.
WE TURN RIGHT HERE.
OKAY!
SUMMIT: 2 KM
DASH
SORRY! ARE YOU TIRED? WANT TO STOP FOR A BIT?
NOPE, I'M FINE! I'VE GOT PLENTY OF STAMINA!
I'M JUST SLOW. SORRY ABOUT THAT.
THIS ISN'T MUCH OF A PICNIC.
IT'S MORE LIKE MOUNTAIN CLIMBING.

I DIDN'T TALK TO SUNA THIS TIME...
MAYBE I MADE A MISTAKE ...?
...
OH, SORRY!
mountain
I'M HAVING SO MUCH FUN THAT I STARTED HUMMING!
YAMATO...
I BET THE FOOD WILL TASTE AMAZING UP ON TOP OF THE MOUNTAIN.
I REALLY LOVE YOU!
IT SURE GETS HOT WITH ALL THIS WALKING, THOUGH!
YOU'RE RIGHT.
mountain

SWOOP
?!
OH!
TAKEO GAVE ME THAT! GET BACK HERE!
NOOOO!
GRAB
DRP

YAMATO!!

GRAB

YAMATO'S FOOD!!

GRAB

MY FLOWER CROWN!

OOOOOO!!!!

EEEEEEK!
SKRITTCH
WHOA !!!
BOMF!
THUD

T-TAKEO!
ARE YOU ALL RIGHT?! TALK TO ME—!
I'M FINE. I SAVED THE FOOD TOO.
mountain
BUT...
...THERE'S NO WAY WE CAN CLIMB BACK UP.
WHERE ARE WE?
mountain
WE NEED TO CALL FOR HELP!
NO SERVICE
...!!
WE'RE OUT OF RANGE, TAKEO!
WHAT?!
...
mountain

WE GOT STRANDED DURING A PICNIC?!
CAW!
CAW!
CAW!
MEANWHILE, YAMATO'S FRIENDS...
WHAT'S RINKO UP TO TODAY?
SHE SAID SHE AND TAKEO WERE GOING ON A PICNIC!
THAT TOTALLY SOUNDS LIKE SOMETHING THEY'D DO.
HER BOY-FRIEND'S SO GREAT.
THEY'VE BEEN GOING OUT FOR ABOUT TWO MONTHS, RIGHT?
SUNAKAWA'S COOL, BUT HE SEEMED HARD TO CONNECT WITH.
HE DIDN'T SAY ANY-THING!
RIGHT?
RINKO'S BOYFRIEND ISN'T EXACTLY *COOL*, BUT...
HMM... HOW SHOULD I PUT THIS?
HE'S VERY MANLY.
THAT SOUNDS GOOD.
I'D SAY HE'S COOL, BUT... WELL...
I GET THE FEELING RINKO THINKS HE LOOKS EVEN COOLER THAN SUNAKAWA.
YEAH.
SHE DEFINITELY DOES.

MEAN-WHILE, THE GODAS ...
DARLING...
HOW ARE YOU FEELING?
VROOO
HUH? I'M FINE.
VROO
ROOOO
THAT'S GOOD.
WHERE'S TAKEO?
HE'S BEEN GONE ALL DAY.
LIFT YOUR FEET, DEAR.
HE'S PROBABLY WITH SUNAKAWA.
VROOO
VROOO
VROOO
ROOO
ROOO
ROOOO
HE'LL BE HOME EVENTUALLY.
OKAY.
VROOO
ROOO
MEAN-WHILE, SUNAKAWA ...
...
BOOK 1
BOOK 2
...

RUSTLE
mountain
THERE AREN'T ANY SIGNS OF ANYONE PASSING THROUGH HERE BEFORE ...
I'M SORRY, TAKEO.
THIS IS MY FAU—
DON'T WORRY! WE'LL MANAGE!
Ountain
WAIT RIGHT HERE.
I'M GOING TO LOOK FROM ABOVE.
HUH?
ABOVE?

GRIP
IF I'D GRABBED A TREE, WE WOULDN'T HAVE FALLEN.
SKFF
SKFF
SKFF
SKFF
BUT...
...THERE'S NO POINT THINKING "WHAT IF."
BE CAREFUL, TAKEO!
mountain
RIGHT NOW, THE MAIN THING IS...
...GETTING YAMATO HOME SAFELY!
FWMP
mountain
IT'LL BE FINE, YAMATO.
WE CAN GET HOME.
WE CAN?

I COULD HEAR FAINT TRAFFIC SOUNDS. THERE'S A ROAD THAT WAY!
REALLY? THAT'S AMAZING, TAKEO!
BUT IT'S PRETTY FAR OFF.
WE MIGHT NOT MAKE IT BACK TO TOWN UNTIL TOMORROW.
WHAT?
SO WE'LL BE...
...SPENDING THE NIGHT TOGETHER?
YEAH.
...
RIGHT...
YAMATO SEEMS UNCOMFORTABLE.
SPENDING
THE NIGHT

TH-THMP
PAT
DON'T WORRY ABOUT A THING.
JUST LEAVE EVERYTHING TO ME.
SQUEEE
FIRST, WE HEAD DUE SOUTH.
FOLLOW ME WHILE I BREAK A TRAIL.
WE DON'T HAVE TO MOVE TOO FAST, BUT WE SHOULD TRAVEL WHILE IT'S LIGHT OUT.
IS SOUTH THAT WAY?!
UM...
OKAY!
RUSTLE
RUSTLE
SNAP
SWISH
SKFF
SNAP
YANK
CRACK

ARE YOU HOLDING UP?
IF YOU FEEL LIKE YOU'RE FALLING BEHIND, YOU CAN GRAB MY SHIRT.
TOSS
TOSS
EEEEE!
GROWL GROWL
GUR
GURGLE
LET'S STOP AND EAT, TAKEO!
WOW!
THANKS, YAMATO!
IT'S DELICIOUS!
CHOMP
CHOMP
REALLY? OH, I'M SO GLAD!
COOKING'S NOT REALLY MY FORTE...

EATING OUTSIDE IS SO MUCH FUN THOUGH!
YEAH!
LET'S SAVE HALF OF THE FOOD FOR TONIGHT.
IT WAS SUPER GOOD!
CLAP!
...
TO-NIGHT...
C'MON! LET'S COVER AS MUCH GROUND AS WE CAN BEFORE SUNSET.
O-OKAY...
TONIGHT...
TH-THMP TH-THMP TH-THMP
SHE MUST BE GETTING NERVOUS. I WANT TO HELP HER RELAX...

WE CAN'T REALLY SEE WHERE WE'RE GOING ANYMORE.
LET'S CAMP HERE.
ALREADY?!
SHUP SHUP
mountain
...
HERE, I MADE YOU A BED!
PAT PAT
FWIP
SLEEPING OUTSIDE ...
...WITH TAKEO...!
IT'LL BE FINE.
I'LL BE RIGHT HERE WITH YOU.
AAH

SWSH
MOSQUITO.
mountain
I WON'T LET THEM BITE HER!
TH-THMP TH-THMP TH-THMP TH-THMP TH-THMP TH-THMP
WOW ...!
ARE WE STILL OUT OF CELL RANGE, YAMATO?
HUH?
UM... YEAH. NO SIGNAL.
I SEE... EVERYONE MUST BE WORRIED.

I'M SO SORRY ...
INCOMING CALL
WHO COULD THAT BE?
HELLO?
OH, MRS. YAMATO!
YES! GOOD EVENING!
YES...
YES...
WHAT?!
YOU'RE LOOKING FOR RINKO?!
YOU WANT TO KNOW IF SHE'S WITH US?
...
SHE HASN'T COME HOME FROM HER DATE
EQUALS
SPENDING THE NIGHT TOGETHER!

SHE...
SHE'S RIGHT HERE!
AT MY PLACE!
A WHOLE BUNCH OF US ARE HERE!
LYING FOR FRIENDS
OH, RIGHT NOW?
SHE'S... IN THE BATHROOM!
YES! DON'T WORRY.
WE'RE HAVING A SLEEPOVER!
YES!
YES!
END
AAAAHHHHHHHHH
WHAT'S GOING ON, RINKO?!
SERIOUSLY?!
SO FAST!!
EEEEEEEEE!!
I'VE GOTTA CALL HER...
...AND SAY WE COVERED FOR HER!
WHAAT?!
HEY!
SHE'S NOT PICKING UP!
WHAT GIVES?
EEEEE!
I'LL TEXT HER!
OH MY GOD!

MEAN-WHILE, THE GODAS ...
DARLING...
HOW ARE YOU—?
I'M FINE.
TAKEO'S NOT BACK YET.
DON'T WORRY.
HE'LL BE HOME EVEN-TUALLY.
OKAY.
IF HE DOESN'T WANT DINNER, HE CAN EAT IT TOMORROW MORNING.
I'LL SET SOME ASIDE.
MEAN-WHILE, SUNAKAWA ...
...
...
SHUT
CLICK

IT'S SO DARK IN THE MOUNTAINS AT NIGHT...
YEAH.
...
THANKS FOR THE FOOD!
mountain
...
TAKEO...
UM...
CAN I HOLD YOUR HAND?
SURE!
EEEEEE!
CLUTCH
SHE STILL SEEMS NERVOUS ...
mountain

?! EEEEP! SOME-THING'S COMING!
DMP DMP DMP DMP DMP
GLINT
GRAB
HAH!
mountain

WH-WHAT WAS THAT?!
A BEAR?!
IT'S NOTHING. JUST A WILD BOAR.
A W-WILD—
THMP
WHUP
IT'S OKAY.
I'M RIGHT HERE.
T-TAKEO...
SHE SOUNDS SCARED...

DON'T WORRY, YAMATO.
mountain
I'D FIGHT EVEN A BEAR FOR YOU.
WOW...
I'LL PROTECT YOU.
LOOK!
THE MOON'S BRIGHT NOW!
HUH? OH! YOU'RE RIGHT!
I BET THE EXTRA LIGHT WILL HELP HER CALM DOWN.
THANK YOU, MOON!

YOU MUST BE EXHAUSTED BY NOW.
LET'S LIE DOWN.
EH?
ROLL
...
AHHH!
ROLL
CHECK OUT THE SKY, YAMATO. THE STARS ARE BEAUTIFUL.
HUH?
OH! YOU'RE RIGHT!
IT'S SO DARK OUT HERE THAT WE CAN SEE MILLIONS OF THEM!
YEAH!

IT'S LIKE A PLANETARIUM!
YEAH, IT IS.
HUH?
ARE YOU WORRIED?
NOPE, I'M OKAY.
YOU KEEP CHECKING TO SEE IF I'M ALL RIGHT, BUT I'M TOTALLY FINE.
I'M SO HAPPY RIGHT NOW.
ARE YOU FEELING ALL RIGHT, YAMATO?
THAT'S GOOD.
YEAH.

THIS IS SO GREAT...
ACTUALLY...
...I THINK I'D BE HAPPY TO LIVE IN THESE MOUNTAINS WITH YOU FOR THE REST OF MY LIFE...
UGA UGA!
UGA!
UGA!
EEEE!
...
T-TAKEO?

ZZZ
OH MY GOSH, I GET TO SEE HIM SLEEP!
YAY! YAY! YAAY!
SORRY, TAKEO...
YOU GOT EXHAUSTED WHILE TAKING CARE OF ME...
AND HERE I AM GETTING ALL EXCITED ...
I LOVE YOU, TAKEO.
I LOVE YOU A LOT.

EEEEEEP!
untain
SMOOCH
mo

mountain
SCRATCH
SCRATCH
SCRATCH
SCRATCH
SCRATCH
SCRATCH
SCRATCH
...
OH!
IS YAMATO SAFE?!
SHUP

ZZZ
ZZZ
mountain
I GET TO SEE HER SLEEP.
DID SHE FALL ASLEEP BECAUSE SHE FEELS SAFE BEING WITH ME?
GOOD MORNING, TAKEO!
I LOVE HER.

OH! LOOK, TAKEO!
LOOK AT ALL THE LITTLE ANIMALS!
HMM?
THEY MUST FEEL SO SAFE AND RELAXED AROUND YOU!
THEY'RE SO CUTE!
REALLY?
mountain
YEAH!
I SEE.
THAT'S GOOD.
mountain

WE FOUND A ROAD!
WE MADE IT!
ARE YOU HURT ANYWHERE, YAMATO?!
Ountain
NOPE! I'M FINE.
JUST ITCHY.
WHAT ?!

GAH...
I COULDN'T PROTECT HER...!
OH NO! TAKEO, THE MOSQUITOES ATE YOU ALIVE!
YEAH, I ATTRACT THEM FOR SOME REASON.
YOU DO?
WELL, THAT MEANS I MANAGED TO LURE AT LEAST ONE OF THEM AWAY FROM YOU!
YAMATO...
GO ME! ♪
I'M GLAD! ♡
mounta

YOU'RE THE BEST.
VROOOM
THERE'S A BUS.
I SHOULD CALL HOME RIGHT AWAY.
mountain
HUH? I HAVE A MESSAGE FROM NANAKO.
Rinko~~~!!!!
I made up an excuse for your mom!
Come to my place tomorrow.
We expect a full report!
No details spared!
We'll all be waiting!
?
STATION
WELL...
I'M GUESS I'M GOING TO NANAKO'S.
OKAY.
SAY HI FOR ME.
I WILL!
mount
WHAT IS IT?

AFTER SPENDING THIS MUCH TIME WITH YOU, GOING OUR SEPARATE WAYS AGAIN MAKES ME SAD.
YAMATO...
SEE YOU LATER, TAKEO!
I FEEL THE SAME WAY.

HEY!
RINKO'S HERE!
WE STAYED UP WAITING FOR YOU!
COME IN, COME IN!
UM... THANKS FOR INVITING ME?
?
SO? HOW WAS IT?
TH-THMP TH-THMP TH-THMP TH-THMP TH-THMP TH-THMP TH-THMP
HUH?
ANYWAY, YOU'RE FILTHY!
SERIOUSLY, WHAT HAPPENED?
WE KINDA GOT STRANDED.
WHAT?!
AND THERE WAS A WILD BOAR!
WHAT?
I THOUGHT I WAS GONNA DIE...
WHAT?!
NO WAY!
YIKES
BUT SINCE TAKEO WAS WITH ME, I FELT SAFE! ♡
EEEEEE

I'M HOME!
HOW ARE YOU FEELING, MOM?
WELCOME HOME.
I'M FINE.
WHERE WERE YOU?
UP IN THE MOUNTAINS.
SIP
YOU WERE, HUH?
WERE YOU WORRIED?
NOT PARTICULARLY.
THAT'S GOOD.
DING!

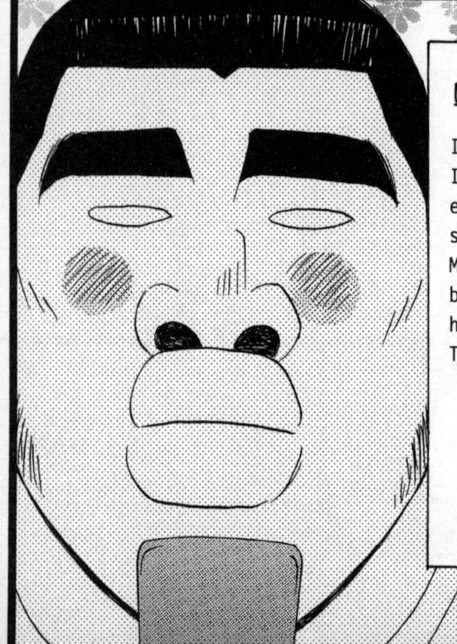

From Yamato

I'm glad we got home safely!
I'm sorry for being so excited when you were working so hard.
My heart was pounding from being alone with you, but I had a lot of fun!
Thank you, Takeo.

SLAM!
mountain
SUNA!
TEACH ME HOW TO DO EMOTICONS!
...
(STILL SLEEPING)
...WHAT?
I CAN'T PUT MY FEELINGS FOR YAMATO INTO WORDS.
UH... WHAT KIND OF FEELINGS?
IT'S LIKE...

BANG
AND...
BOOM
AND...
FWOOM
AND...
SWOOSH
AND...
OH... THAT'S NICE.
TAKEO...
BONG AND...
...ZOOM AND...
...THUDUDUD AND FOOF AND...
HEY, TAKEO?
I DON'T THINK EMOTICONS ARE UP TO THE JOB.
I LOVE YOU SO MUCH...
...YAMATO!!

MY love STORY!!

MY FRIENDS AND I WERE TALKING ABOUT GOING TO THE BEACH WITH YOU AND *YOUR* FRIENDS!

THE BEACH?

YEAH!

MAKE SURE YOU INVITE SUNAKAWA!

DOES THAT SOUND FUN? HOW ABOUT SUNAKAWA?

IT SOUNDS FANTASTIC!
YEAH! LET'S GO!
THE BEACH, HUH?
THE OCEAN IS HUGE.
IT'S A GOOD PLACE.
WHAT? GOING TO THE BEACH WITH TAKEO'S GIRLFRIEND'S FRIENDS?!
I WANT TO GO.
COUNT ME IN TOO!
I'M DRAG-GING YOU, SUNA.
HUH?
IT'LL BE FUN TO GO WITH YAMATO.
HEHHEHEH...♥
I CAN'T WAIT TO SEE THE GIRLS' SWIMSUITS!
NOT YOU.
YOU'RE NOT COMING!
HUH?
WHY?

SWIM-SUITS...
...ARE JUST CLOTHES FOR SWIMMING!
ARE'NT YOU LOOKING FORWARD TO SEEING WHAT YOUR GIRLFRIEND WEARS?
HUH? WHAT'RE YOU TALKING ABOUT? GIRLS' SWIMSUITS ARE HALF THE FUN OF GOING TO THE BEACH.
HE'S RIGHT!
YAMATO WOULD ONLY WEAR A SWIMSUIT MEANT FOR SWIMMING!
I REFUSE TO BE SOME SCUMBAG WHO GIVES HER WEIRD LOOKS!
...
DON'T WORRY, YAMATO.
IT DOESN'T MATTER WHAT KIND OF SWIMSUIT YOU WEAR.
...

WHAT SHOULD I GET?
OOH, THIS IS CUTE!
LUCKY YOU, WITH YOUR BIG BOOBS.
WELL, YOU'VE GOT GREAT LEGS!
WHAT ABOUT THIS ONE?
TA-DA!
?!
SO HIGH-CUT...
NO, HUH?
MAYBE THIS, THEN?
TA-DA!
...
W-WELL, THEN...
THIS ONE ...?!
WHAT'S GOTTEN INTO YOU, RINKO?
HUH?!
I-IT'S JUST THAT...
...TAKEO'S SO COOL, YOU KNOW?
HUH ?!

WELL, I GUESS...
IT MAKES SENSE THAT YOU THINK THAT.
I'M LIKE A LITTLE KID COMPARED TO HIM!
THAT'S NOT TRUE...
HE'S SO WELL PROPOR-TIONED, AND I'M JUST NOT—!
I WOULDN'T SAY "COOL"...
HE DOESN'T EVEN LOOK LIKE HE'S IN HIGH SCHOOL. HE'S SO MUSCULAR!
HE'S LIKE AN OLYMPIC POWER-LIFTER.
I WONDER WHAT RINKO'S BOYFRIEND WILL WEAR?
AH HA HA HA
HE MIGHT JUST WEAR SCHOOL SWIM TRUNKS.
GAH
OR MAYBE THOSE SPORTY BRIEFS.
THE ONES THAT DON'T COVER ANYTHING!
HE'D TOTALLY WEAR THAT FOR SWIMMING!
HA HA
HA HA HA
LOOK...
I'M ALWAYS SO EXCITED WHEN I SEE HIM...
SO I WANT *HIM* TO BE EXCITED WHEN HE LOOKS AT *ME*!
I WANT TO DO MY BEST!
THAT'D BE SO AMAZING!
OH MY GOSH!
...

MAKES SENSE...
YOU'RE RIGHT!
YOU WANT TO GET YOUR BOY-FRIEND EXCITED!
YOU DEF-INITELY WANT HIM TO THINK YOU'RE CUTE!
LET'S ALL CHOOSE A SWIMSUIT FOR RINKO!
YEAH!
THIS IS GOOD.
WHAT?!
HOW ABOUT THIS?
THAT'LL DAZZLE HIM!
WHAT ABOUT THIS?
THAT'S PERFECT.
TAKEO...
THE FORECAST IS CALLING FOR A TYPHOON. WILL WE BE ALL RIGHT TOMORROW?
I'M AT HIS PLACE GETTING READY RIGHT NOW.
A TYPHOON?
YOU MAKE THE SUN SHINE, SO IT SHOULD BE FINE.
SUNA SAYS I'LL MAKE THE SUN SHINE, SO WE'LL BE FINE.
HA HA! IS THAT RIGHT?

I'M GETTING READY TOO. I'M REALLY LOOKING FORWARD TO IT!
YEAH, I AM TOO.
WELL, SEE YOU TO-MORROW!
SEE YOU THEN.
UM, TAKEO?
WHAT IS THAT?
WATERMELONS! WE'RE PLAYING THAT SPLITTING-WATERMELONS GAME, RIGHT?
THAT LOOKS LIKE A LOT. HOW MANY ARE IN THERE?
AND WOULDN'T IT BE BETTER TO BLOW UP THE INFLATABLE STUFF ONCE YOU GET THERE? THEY'RE TAKING UP A LOT OF SPACE.
OH, GOTCHA.
BOAT
TUBE
BEACH BALL
TAKEO, ARE YOU REALLY ALL RIGHT?
WHAT DO YOU MEAN?
...NOTH-ING.
WORRIED ABOUT THE WEATHER?
...
NEVER MIND.

I LOVE THE BEACH.

AS A KID, I WAS BLOWN AWAY WATCHING THE OCEAN SUNSET.

I WANT TO WATCH THE SUNSET THERE WITH YAMATO.

OKAY!

SEA
IT'S SO SUNNY!
TOTALLY!
IT'S BEEN AGES, GUYS!
HOW'VE YOU BEEN?
HOW'RE WE GETTING THERE? TRAIN? BUS?
TAKING THE BUS.
WANT SOME CANDY?
HOW DID YOU DO ON THE SEMESTER EXAM?
WHY THE HECK WOULD YOU ASK THAT?!

WHAT'S WRONG, YAMATO? ARE YOU TOO WARM?
HUH? NO! OH! YEAH!
YAMATO...
...SURE IS CUTE.
TH-THMP TH-THMP TH-THMP TH-THMP
HE'S SO CLOSE TO ME...
ZZSSSSH
SPLISH
SHOULD WE PUT THE UMBRELLA UP HERE?
SHOULD WE RENT ANOTHER ONE?
THAT'S AMAZING, TAKEO!
YOU BLEW IT UP IN ONE BREATH!
PUFF
WHERE ARE THE GIRLS?
CHANGING.

SWIMSUITS!!!
WOOHOO!
GLARE
THE BEACH IS FOR...
...SWIMMING, SPLITTING WATERMELONS AND HUNTING CRABS.
THERE THEY ARE!
THANKS FOR WAIT-ING!

ZZZSSSHH
SPLASH
STOP STARING LIKE THAT.
WHY DON'T YOU CHANGE INTO YOUR SWIMSUIT, TAKEO?
YOU'RE ALL SO CUTE!
HUH? HA HA.. HA...
OH!
YEAH! I PROBABLY SHOULD!
YOU'RE ACTING LIKE A DIRTY OLD MAN. HA HA...

TA-DA!
TH-THMP
TH-THMP
TH-THMP
TH-THMP
TH-THMP

DAYS AT THE BEACH ARE ABOUT...

...HUNTING CRABS...

...DIGGING FOR CLAMS...

...SPLIT-TING WATER-MELONS...

...SWIM-MING AS HARD AS YOU CAN...

BLUB
...GETTING WEIRD SUNTANS...
BLUB
...HAVING YOUR SKIN PEEL LIKE A MAP...
BLUB
...ENTERING A SUNTAN CONTEST AT THE END OF SUMMER...
BLUB
BLUB
...AND WINNING!
WHY DOES IT FEEL SO STRANGE TODAY?
A SEA MON-STER?!
IT'S SO WEIRD. I CAN'T GO NEAR HER!
THAT WHALE OFF-SHORE IS HIM, RIGHT?
...
RINKO, DON'T YOU THINK TAKEO'S PRETTY FAR OUT?
DAZED
TAKEO!
YOU LOOK SO GOOD IN THE SUN!
NOW'S NOT THE TIME TO GET CAPTIVATED BY HIM!
DON'T YOU WANT TO GET HIM EXCITED?
TAKE THAT HOODIE OFF!
HUH? O-OKAY.

I JUST HAVE TO MAKE SURE I DON'T LOOK AT HER–!
SPLIT THE WATER-MELON!
WRONG WAY, TAKEO!
BWA HA HA!
?!
HOW FAR IS HE GONNA GO?
HA HA HA!
LEFT, LEFT!
GREAT! NOW STRAIGHT FORWARD.
THREE MORE STEPS...
SO COOL
DAZED—
OH!
WAIT, TAKEO!
STOP!
THAT'S YAMATO...!

YANK
WHAT ?!

GOOD GRIEF, RINKO! STOP ZONING OUT!
O-OKAY...
FWISH
CALM DOWN, TAKEO.
SHE'S JUST WEARING CLOTHING.

CLOTHING ?!
THAT'S RIGHT.
CLOTHING TO WEAR IN THE WATER.
CLOTHING, HUH?
I JUST HAVE TO THINK OF IT AS CLOTH-ING.
IT'S CLOTHING MEANT FOR SWIMMING THAT DOESN'T COVER VERY MUCH.
CLOTHES !!...
IT DOESN'T COVER MUCH...
FOR SWIM-MING...
GOT IT? HAVE YOU CALMED DOWN?
OKAY, THEN GO.
CLOTHES!
GRP
THAT'S RIGHT.
TAKEO IS BACK IN THE GAME!!!
SORRY TO KEEP YOU WAITING, YAMATO!
YAMATO! THE BEACH IS A GREAT PLACE.
LET'S HAVE TONS OF FUN!

ALL RIGHT!
TIME FOR SOME BEACH VOLLEY-BALL!
O...
OKAY!
YEAH!
349...
YARGH!
HUP!
355...
...

362...
363...
364...
YOU'RE SO COOL, TAKEO!
WHEEZE...
WHEEZE...
WHEEZE...
WHEEZE...
WHEEZE...
RINKO'S BOYFRIEND HITS THE BALL PERFECTLY EVERY TIME!
WE'RE DRAWING A CROWD!
DROPOUTS
HE'S...A MACHINE...
THERE YOU GO!
TOSS
WHEE!
SPLASH
OKAY!
THROW ME NEXT, TAKEO!
ME TOO!
SPLOOSH
WANT ME TO THROW YOU TOO, YAMATO?

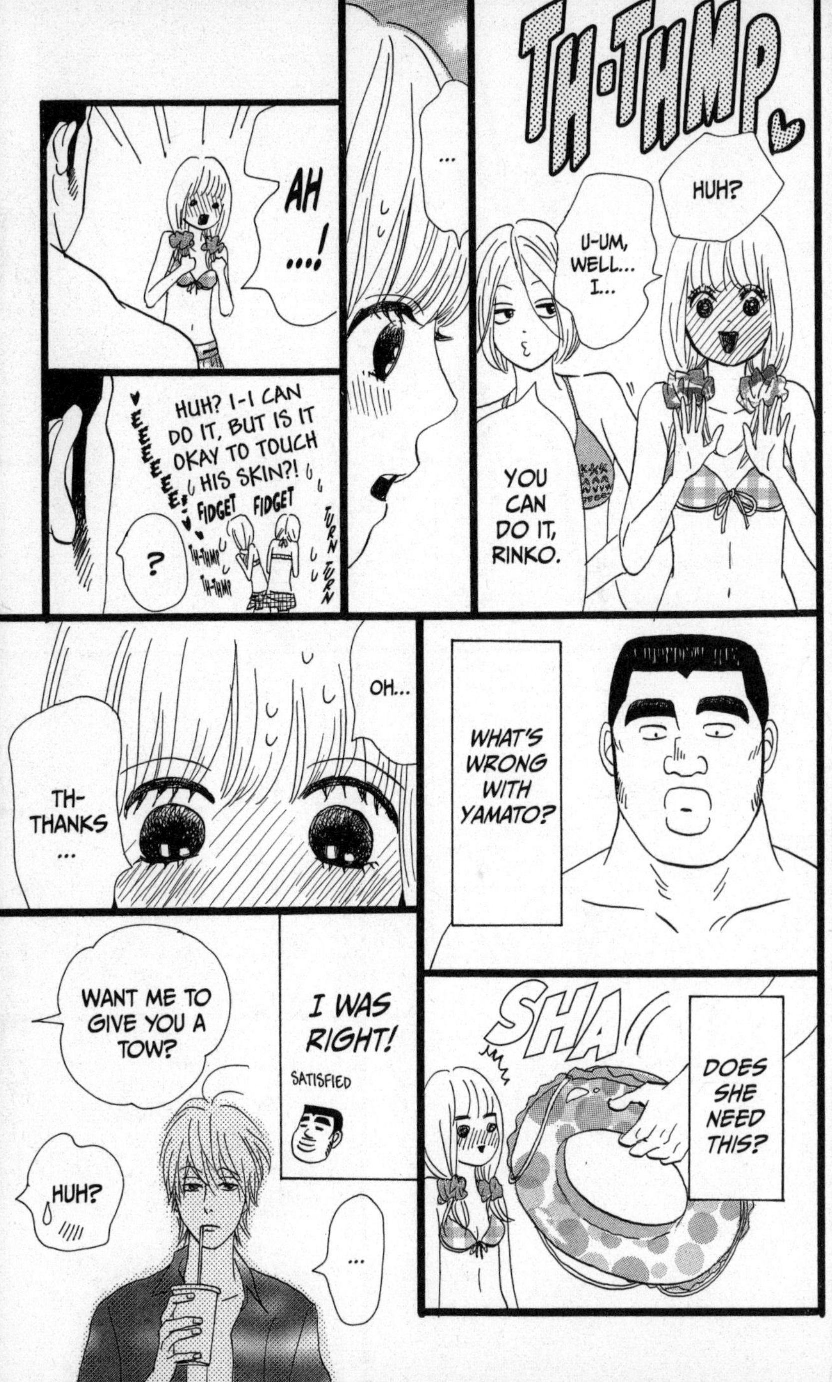
TH-THMP
HUH?
U-UM, WELL... I...
YOU CAN DO IT, RINKO.
...
AH ...!
HUH? I-I CAN DO IT, BUT IS IT OKAY TO TOUCH HIS SKIN?!
FIDGET FIDGET
TURN TURN
TH-THMP TH-THMP
?
WHAT'S WRONG WITH YAMATO?
OH...
TH-THANKS ...
SHA
DOES SHE NEED THIS?
I WAS RIGHT!
SATISFIED
WANT ME TO GIVE YOU A TOW?
HUH?
...

KYAAA!
YOU'RE SO FAST, TAKEO!
HA HA HA HA
WOW, THAT LOOKS FUN!
THERE YOU GO!
SPIN
GYA HA
SPIN
HA
SPIN
HA
SPIN
HA
HA
HA
WA
HA
SPIN
HA
HA
HEY, TAKEO?
HMM?

KYAH!
HA HA HA HA!
OH?
WHO'S THAT GUY THE KIDS ARE PLAYING WITH?
HE HAS AN AMAZING BODY!
ALL THOSE MUSCLES!
YEAH, HE'S NOTHING LIKE MY HUSBAND.
HEE HEE!
HE'S GOT WASH-BOARD ABS!
TH-THMP
TAKEO'S AWFULLY POPULAR ...
YAMATO! WANT TO GET OUT?
SPLASH
CROWD GATHERING
WOW!
AMAZING!
S-SURE ...
TH-THMP TH-THMP
HE REALLY, REALLY IS!

BEACH SHAC
WELCOM
RINKO, THERE'S CORN STUCK IN YOUR TEETH.
OH, NO!
MUNCH MUNCH
MUNCH
BLINK
TH-THMP
YAMATO...
WHY'S SHE SQUIRMING LIKE THAT?
EEEE! EEEE!
PANIC PANIC
THAT'S SO CUTE.
I WANT TO GET HIM EXCITED, BUT I KEEP BEING THE ONE WHO GETS ALL WORKED UP.
YOU REALLY LIKE HIM, DON'T YOU?
PANT PANT PANT
WHY DON'T YOU GO GET COZY WITH HIM?
RINKO?! SHE'D PROBABLY HAVE A HEART ATTACK!
...

STAND
I'M GOING TO GIVE IT A TRY!
EXCUSE ME, LADIES.
WOW, GOOD LUCK!
YOU SURE EAT A LOT.
TH-THMP
TH-THMP
TH-THMP
TH-THMP
TH-THMP
TH-THMP
TURN!
TH-TH-THMP
Grilled Corn ¥500
WHAT'S WRONG, YAMATO?

TAKEO ...?
UM... ER...
WANT TO GO HANG OUT BY THE ROCKS WITH ME?
BY THE ROCKS!
NOD!
I BET SHE WANTS TO GO HUNT CRABS! THAT'S A GREAT SPOT!
YOU BET!
...

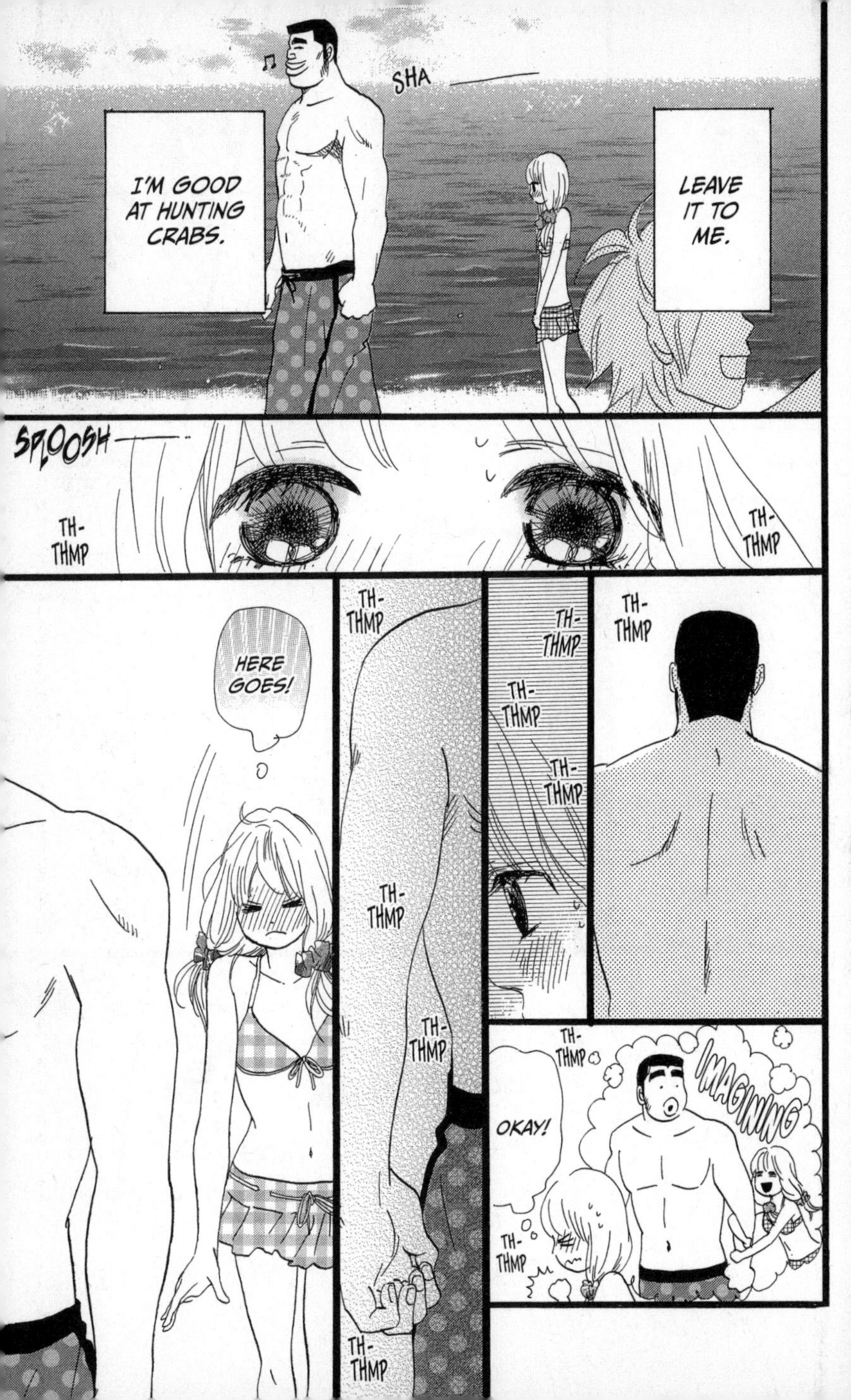

LEAVE IT TO ME.
SHA
I'M GOOD AT HUNTING CRABS.
SPLOOSH
TH-THMP
TH-THMP
TH-THMP
TH-THMP
TH-THMP
TH-THMP
TH-THMP
TH-THMP
TH-THMP
TH-THMP
IMAGINING
OKAY!
TH-THMP
HERE GOES!

REACH
LOOK OUT, YAMATO.
YOU'RE GOING TO STEP ON THAT.
OH...
BLUSH
I...
I'M SORRY, TAKEO!
I WAS ONLY THINKING ABOUT MYSELF.
THIS IS SO EMBARRASSING!
I'M SORRY!
DASH
YAMATO?!
SMOOSH

OH.
SORRY.
PAT PAT
YOU SURE ARE CLUMSY.
SUNA!
HURRY UP AND GO AFTER HER. I'LL TAKE CARE OF THIS.
PAT PAT
THANKS, SUNA!
NO BIGGIE.

YAMATO!
OH, TAKEO...
WHAT'S THE MATTER?
UM... IT'S JUST...
I'M JUST SO *EMBARRASSED*.
YOU WERE COMPLETELY AWARE OF YOUR SURROUNDINGS...
...BUT I WAS ALL WRAPPED UP IN MYSELF.
IT'S SO EMBARRASSING. I'M NO USE TODAY.
HUH? I DIDN'T DO ANYTHING SPECIAL.

IS IT OKAY IF I SIT DOWN?
HUH?
S-SURE!
SHOOSH
SPLASH
WHAT A GREAT SUNSET.
YEAH, IT'S GORGEOUS!
AHH, THAT'S RIGHT.
I WAS REALLY HOPING...
...TO SEE THE SUNSET WITH HER TODAY.
I'M GLAD WE GOT TO DO THIS.

I'M SO HAPPY RIGHT NOW.

IT'S SO BEAUTIFUL...

SHA SHAA

...

SPLSSSH

I'VE ALWAYS WANTED ...

...TO BECOME SOMEONE WHO'S AS BIG-HEARTED...
...AS THE OCEAN.

AND I WANT TO BE WITH YOU.

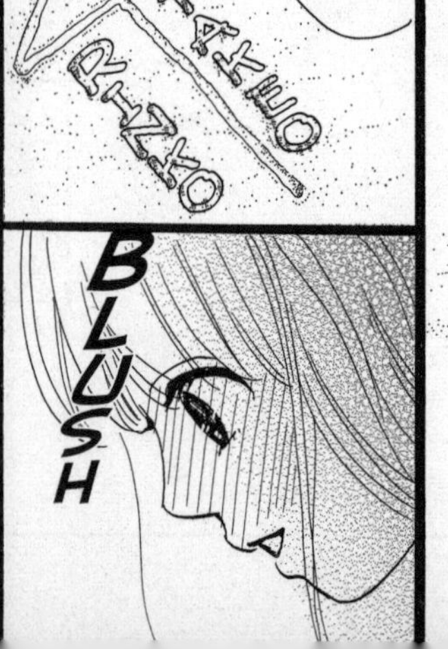

YAMATO
...
YOU'RE BEAUTIFUL.
SHAA
TAKEO
RINKO
OH!
GUARD!
IT'LL BE FINE!
THANK YOU!

MAYBE IT'S THE WARMTH OF THE SETTING SUN...
SPLASH
...MAKING MY FACE FEEL SO HOT.
MY CHEST FEELS HOT TOO.

YAMATO...
I LOVE YOU.
MM-HMM.

SAME HERE.
SPLASH
I LOVE YOU TOO, TAKEO.
TH-THMP
ZSSSSH
TH-THMP
YAMATO...
SPLOOSH

SPLASH
I...
I...
TH-THMP TH-THMP TH-THMP
OH, HEY!
SO THIS IS WHERE YOU TWO GOT TO! WHAT'RE YOU DOING?
WE'RE GOING TO SET OFF FIRE-WORKS!
C'MON, HURRY UP!
...

SIZZLE
OH, I SEE.
SO YOU DIDN'T MANAGE TO GET HIM ALL EXCITED.
NOPE.
AND YOU TRIED SO HARD TOO...
BUT I DID HAVE A LOT OF FUN!
YEAH, THIS WAS A GOOD DAY.
WANNA GO WATCH FIREWORKS WITH EVERYBODY SOMETIME?
WE COULD WEAR YUKATAS!
YEAH!
YUKATAS?
DO YOU THINK TAKEO WOULD LIKE SEEING ME IN A YUKATA?!
LET IT GO, RINKO.

SUNA...

THIS WAS A REALLY EMOTIONAL DAY.

WATCHING THE SUNSET WITH YAMATO WAS AMAZING.

YEAH? THAT'S GOOD.

IT WAS GREAT!

HEY, TAKEO!

WE WERE THINKING OF ALL GOING TO SEE FIRE-WORKS SOMETIME! SOUND GOOD?

FIREWORKS, HUH? THAT SOUNDS GREAT! LET'S DO IT!

I'LL GET HIM WORKED UP NEXT TIME!

YAMATO AND FIRE-WORKS...! NOW THAT WOULD BE EMOTIONAL ...!

...

MY
Love
STORY!!

WERE YOU WAITING LONG, TAKEO?
NOPE! I JUST GOT HERE MYSELF!
THUMBS UP!
HYBRID
...
HYBRID
NOOOO!

DO YOU WANNA GO SEE A MOVIE, SUNAKAWA?
YEAH! YOU LIKE BOOKS AND MOVIES AND STUFF!
I DON'T HAVE MUCH MONEY RIGHT NOW.
THAT'S PER-FECT!
IT IS?
IGNORE WHAT I JUST SAID!
IT'S MY TREAT! I JUST GOT PAID!
LET'S GO!
UH... THANKS. I'LL PAY YOU BACK.
CINEMA
WHICH ONE DO YOU WANT TO SEE?
PICK WHICHEVER SOUNDS BEST!

...
GO ON, GO ON, GO ON, GO ON!
MAYBE THIS ONE?
...
YOU LIAR!
LOVE COMEDY
DON'T THINK ABOUT US. TODAY YAMATO AND I WANT TO SEE WHAT **YOU** WANT TO SEE!
UH-HUH!
...
THEN... THIS ONE?
OKAY!
DID YOU REALLY SEE WHO DID IT?
I DID! I'M TELLING THE TRUTH!

TAKEO...

SUNA!

HOW WAS THE MOVIE?!

WAS IT GOOD?!

THEY CHANGED THE ENDING FROM THE ORIGINAL, BUT I ENJOYED IT.

WAS IT INTER-ESTING?

YEAH, WAS IT INTER-ESTING?!

HUH? YEAH, IT WAS INTER-ESTING.

ALL RIGHT!

NEVER MIND THAT! WHEN DID THE GUILTY DUDE DIE?

WHILE YOU WERE SLEEPING.

THAT WASN'T WHO DID IT.

WERE EITHER OF YOU PAYING ATTENTION?

WOOOW
LOOK, SUNAKAWA! IT'S THE MOUNTAINS!
TAKE A LOOK, SUNA! IT'S THE MOUNTAINS!
YEP.
I SEE THEM.
BRID
DO YOU LIKE THE MOUNTAINS, SUNAKAWA?
MOUNTAINS SURE ARE GREAT.
WHAT DO YOU THINK, SUNA?!
ARE YOU HAVING FUN, SUNAKAWA?
I DON'T COME UP HERE VERY OFTEN, BUT...
...YEAH.

SO YOU'RE HAVING FUN?
UH, YEAH. I AM.
VICTORY!
...
?
HEY, PERFECT TIMING.
LET'S HAVE A QUICK REST OVER THERE!
OKAY.
I'M NOT THAT TIRED THOUGH.
HYBRID
NOD!
SUNA!

HAPPY...
...BIRTH-DAY!!
SUNAKAWA
HUH?
TODAY IS YOUR BIRTHDAY, ISN'T IT?
IT'S SEPTEMBER 13TH, RIGHT?
YEAH, THE 13TH.
YOU'RE RIGHT. TODAY'S MY BIRTHDAY.
HYBRID
...
I'M JUST KINDA SURPRISED. I DIDN'T EXPECT ANY OF THIS.
HEH HEH
AND YOU'RE USUALLY SO SHARP! WE DID AN AMAZING JOB IF YOU DIDN'T NOTICE.

WELL... SINCE I WASN'T EXPECTING IT, I'M NOT SURE HOW TO REACT.
BE HAPPY.
GOOD POINT.
I AM HAPPY.
THANK YOU.
SUCCESS!
HERE'S YOUR PRESENT!
WHAT IS IT?
WHERE WERE YOU HIDING SUCH A HUGE BAG?
IT'S A BLANKET!

YOU GET COLD EASILY, RIGHT? YOU STAY UNDER THE BLANKETS ALL NIGHT.
YOU'RE JUST QUICK TO KICK BLANKETS OFF.
THAT'S BECAUSE I GET HOT EASILY!
SOMETIMES I CAN'T SLEEP BECAUSE MY FEET ARE HOT, SO I REST THEM ON THE WINDOW TO KEEP THEM COOL!
YOUR BODY TEMPERA-TURE'S SO HIGH!
BRID
OKAY.
I'LL USE IT.
THANK YOU.
NO PROBLEM!
IT LOOKS GOOD ON YOU.
...THANKS.

KA-CHUK
KA-CHUK
I'M SO GLAD WE MADE SUNAKAWA HAPPY.
YEAH!
I GET THE FEELING HE WAS PRETTY PLEASED.
IT WAS REALLY FUN!
HYBRID
AT THE THEATER...
HMM?
MY HEART WAS POUNDING FROM SITTING NEXT TO YOU.
WE WERE THERE FOR SUNAKAWA'S BIRTHDAY...
...BUT I WAS SO HAPPY TO BE WITH YOU, I COULD BARELY THINK!
YAMATO...
THMP THMP
I LOVE YOU.
THMP THMP THMP THMP
IS THAT AN EARTHQUAKE?!
THMP THMP THMP THMP

HEY, TAKEO...
TODAY IS OUR FIVE-MONTH ANNIVERSARY!
WE STARTED DATING ON APRIL 13TH.
REALLY?
UH-HUH!
AND I REMEMBER THE DATE WE FIRST HELD HANDS.
I WANT TO CELEBRATE THAT TOO!
I SEE ...!
WHAT DO YOU WANT?
PLEASE LEAVE ME ALONE!
HUH?
IS SOMEONE BOTHERING HER?
SHUP

HEY, YOU—!
YBRID
TAKEO?
HUH?
IT *IS* YOU!
WOW, YOU HAVEN'T CHANGED AT ALL!
OH.
OH NO...
THAT GUY'S BEEN FOLLOWING ME AROUND LATELY.
BUT HE RAN OFF AS SOON AS YOU CAME OVER!
I SHOULD CALL YOU NEXT TIME I HAVE PROBLEMS!
IT'S SATO. WE WERE ON THE STUDENT COUNCIL TOGETHER IN MIDDLE SCHOOL.

SHE WAS IN LOVE WITH SUNA.
SMILE
HOW IS SUNAKAWA DOING?
ARE YOU ALL RIGHT, TAKEO?
?
THIS IS RINKO YAMATO.
OH, HELLO.
NICE TO MEET YOU.
HI. CALL ME SATO.
NICE TO MEET YOU TOO.
...
ARE YOU TWO FRIENDS?
WE WERE ON THE SAME COMMITTEE IN MIDDLE SCHOOL.
COM-MITTEE?

THE PRINTOUT COMMITTEE!
WHAT DID YOU DO?
WE JUST MADE PRINTOUTS.
* WHAT IS THE PRINT-OUT COMMITTEE? * THEIR JOB IS TO PREP PRINT-OUTS FOR THE ENTIRE SCHOOL. THEY COMPILE THE TEACHERS' HANDOUTS, STAPLE THEM TOGETHER AND DELIVER THEM TO EACH CLASSPOOM. THEY HAVE TO WORK OUT THE MOST EFFICIENT METHODS.
HA HA! THAT WAS A STRANGE JOB, WASN'T IT?
SEE YOU AROUND.
OKAY.
GLANCE
THAT GIRL...
...WE MET EARLIER...
WERE YOU ONLY TOGETHER ON THAT COMMITTEE?
HM?
WELL...
I WAS WONDERING IF SHE HAD FEELINGS FOR YOU BACK THEN.
SATO? NO WAY.
SHE DIDN'T LIKE ME, APPARENTLY.
HOW COME?

SUNA TOLD ME...
...SHE SAID BAD STUFF ABOUT ME.
WHAT? SHE DIDN'T SEEM LIKE THAT TYPE.
SUNA DOESN'T LIE.
HE TOLD ME ALL THE GIRLS I FELL IN LOVE WITH WERE LIKE THAT.
OTHER THAN YAMATO.
HUH? SO *YOU* USED TO LIKE *HER*?
BACK THEN, YEAH.
I SEE...
HYBR

OH...

THIS IS BAD.

HM...

EVEN I CAN TELL...

...THAT YAMATO IS UPSET...

...ABOUT WHAT I JUST SAID.

THIS IS AWFUL.

...

SEE YOU, TAKEO.

THANKS FOR WALKING ME HOME.

BYE...

SLAM

THIS IS REALLY BAD.

SUNA!

ROLL ROLL ROLL ROLL!!

...

WHAT'S WRONG?

WHAT WAS THAT ABOUT?

I REALLY MESSED UP!

HUH?

I RAN INTO SATO ON THE TRAIN EARLIER.

SATO?

OH.

...

DID YOU TELL YAMATO THAT YOU USED TO LIKE SATO?
YEAH.
AND YAMATO GOT DEPRESSED.
AH.
I SCREWED UP.
WELL, I DON'T THINK SHE'D WANT YOU TO HIDE IT.
I DON'T EITHER.
I HAD NO INTENTION OF HIDING IT, BUT I THINK I COULD'VE FOUND A BETTER WAY TO TELL HER.
YEAH.
SUNA...
I BET...
...YOU WOULD'VE BEEN ABLE TO SMOOTH THINGS OVER WITH HER.
I NEVER USED TO CARE WHEN GIRLS LIKED SUNA...
...OR IF THEY BAD-MOUTHED ME.
BUT I CAN'T REALLY SAY THAT ANYMORE.
BUT *YOU'RE* THE ONE YAMATO'S IN LOVE WITH.

SHUP
I'M GOING OUT FOR A RUN.
SLAM
I'VE NEVER...
...BEEN IN THE POSITION OF HAVING A GIRL LIKE ME BEFORE.
SO EVEN IF I WAS KINDA STUPID OR DENSE SOME-TIMES...

...IT NEVER RESULTED IN A GIRL I LOVE GETTING HURT.
YOU SURE ARE FAST.
SUNA!
HYBRID

YAMATO...
...REMEMBERS EXACTLY WHEN WE STARTED DATING AND WHEN WE FIRST HELD HANDS.
THAT'S IMPRESSIVE.
IT SEEMS LIKE SOME-THING SHE'D DO.
SHE SAID THOSE ARE DAYS SHE WANTS TO CELEBRATE.
YAMATO CHERISHES EVERY MOMENT.
I REMEMBERED WHAT HAPPENED ON THOSE DAYS...
...BUT IT NEVER WOULD'VE OCCURRED TO ME TO CELEBRATE THEM.
WHEN I MENTIONED THAT YOUR BIRTHDAY IS SEPTEMBER 13TH...
...SHE WAS THE ONE WHO SAID WE SHOULD SURPRISE YOU.

"LET'S DO SOMETHING SPECIAL FOR HIM! HE'S ALWAYS LOOKING AFTER US.
"I'LL BAKE COOKIES!
"HE'S MY BOYFRIEND'S BEST FRIEND! ♡"
YAMATO AND I...
...PLANNED IT ALL TOGETHER.
"WHAT WOULD BE A GOOD PRESENT TO GET HIM?"
"HOW ABOUT A BLANKET?"
WE PICKED OUT A PRESENT FOR YOU.
"WHAT COLOR WOULD HE LIKE?
"YOU'RE RIGHT. THE COLOR COULD BE IMPORTANT."
"LET'S GO WITH RED! IT'S A NICE WARM COLOR."
IT WAS FUN.

"I HOPE HE LIKES IT!"
IT'S FUN BEING WITH HER.
"TAKEO..."
"TAKEO...!"
"TAKEO!"
YAMATO IS SO SWEET AND KIND.
AND I CAN'T STAND...
...THE FACT THAT...
...I HURT HER.

I'M ALWAYS CAUSING PROBLEMS FOR HER.
WHAT I'D SUG-GEST ...
...IS THAT FROM NOW ON, YOU TRY NOT TO HAVE CONTACT WITH GIRLS YOU USED TO LIKE— INCLUDING SATO.
THAT'S SOMETHING YOU COULD DO.
HYBRID
I GET IT.
YEAH! THAT MAKES SENSE!
OKAY, GOT IT!
I WON'T HAVE ANY CONTACT WITH THEM! I'LL CHANGE!

FROM NOW ON, I WON'T SAVE ANY GIRL BUT YAMATO! NOT EVEN IF THEY'RE BEING MOLESTED!
I'LL CALL THE POLICE!
HUH?
UM, THAT'S NOT WHAT—
HE STOLE MY PURSE!
VROOM
YOINK
DAMMIT!

THANK YOU SO MUCH! I-I'D LIKE TO REPAY YOU SOMEHOW!
COULD YOU GIVE ME YOUR NUMBER ...?
I DIDN'T DO ANYTHING.
LEAP
VROOM
MEW! MEW!
FLIP
SCOOP
DASH
TMP TMP TMP TMP
...

NOOO! MY BALLOON!
HYBRID
YOU DON'T THINK BEFORE YOU ACT, DO YOU?
IT'S PURE REFLEX.
THIS'LL BE IMPOSSIBLE.
NO! I CAN CHANGE. I WILL CHANGE!
YAMATO IS NUMBER ONE!
YOU DON'T NEED TO GO THAT FAR. YAMATO UNDERSTANDS PERFECTLY WELL WHAT KIND OF PERSON YOU ARE.
NO.

I'M NOT TRYING TO MAKE HER UNDERSTAND.
I JUST DON'T WANT TO HURT HER.
IT'S ROUGHER ON THE GIVING END...
...THAN THE RECEIVING END, SUNA.
SEE YOU LATER!
YEAH.
TAKEO.
HM?
...
WHAT IS IT?
YOU'VE GROWN UP A LOT SINCE GETTING A GIRLFRIEND.

I DIDN'T REALLY NEED A BLANKET OR WANT TO GO UP TO THE MOUNTAINS.
REALLY?
HYBRID
BUT I WAS HAPPY YOU CELEBRATED MY BIRTHDAY.
YOU DON'T HAVE TO ACT SMART OR BE GOOD AT EVERYTHING.
YOU'RE INCREDIBLY SINCERE—BOTH YOU *AND* YAMATO.
I'M SURE THINGS'LL WORK OUT OKAY.
SUNA!
THANK YOU!
JUST REMEMBER, I'VE NEVER HAD A GIRL-FRIEND.
SO I DON'T KNOW HOW TO ADVISE YOU.
I SEE. YOU'RE SO RIGHT!
YOU SEEM LIKE YOU'VE DATED AT LEAST TEN GIRLS.
YAMATO...

YOU'RE SO IMPORTANT TO ME.
I DON'T EVER WANT TO SEE YOU SAD AGAIN.
HI, TAKEO.
SHE'S ALREADY FEELING DOWN!
I HAVE TO DO SOME-THING.
YAMATO ...
TH-THMP
ARE YOU BOTHERED BY...
...WHAT HAPPENED THE OTHER DAY?
...
CRAP.
OF COURSE SHE'S BOTHERED.
I CAN'T FIND THE RIGHT WORDS ...
I'M SORRY, YAMATO.

I WISH...
...YOU WERE MY FIRST LOVE.
RRIIING
TAKEO, YOU HAVE A CALL.
OH.
HELLO?
HI, TAKEO?
THIS IS SATO.
SATO?!

WHY?
SORRY FOR CALLING LIKE THIS.
I GOT YOUR NUMBER WHEN WE WERE ON STUDENT COUNCIL.
I STILL HAVE IT.
I SEE.
LISTEN...
THAT GUY FROM THE TRAIN IS FOLLOWING ME.
WHAT?!
I'M AT THE CONVENIENCE STORE IN FRONT OF THE PARK RIGHT NOW.
BUT HE'S WAITING FOR ME OUTSIDE THE STORE. I'M TOO SCARED TO LEAVE.
WHAT'S WRONG?
OH!
I CAN'T HAVE CONTACT WITH ANY GIRLS OTHER THAN YAMATO.
IRON-CLAD RULE
IT'S SATO FROM THE OTHER DAY.
THAT GUY IS HARASSING HER AGAIN.
SHE'S IN THE STORE OVER BY THE PARK.
WHAT—?

DON'T WORRY, I'M NOT GOING.
I'LL CALL THE POLICE.
WAIT, WHAT? WHY?
SHE MUST BE TERRIFIED...
...JUST LIKE I WAS.
COME ON, TAKEO!
ARE YOU SURE?
YEAH! LET'S GO!

YAMATO...
...
STALK
STALK
STALK
STALK
STALK
BUMP

...!!!

IT'S...

VOOM

IT'S NOT WHAT YOU THINK! I-I JUST HAPPENED TO SEE HER!

I WON'T DO IT AGAIN! I'M SORRY!

ZOOM

HE RAN AWAY.
WAS THAT HIM?
YEAH.

TAKEO!
YOU CAME!
HEY.
GRIP

BLUSH

Y-YOU GUYS ARE IN LOVE, HUH?

CON-GRATU-LATIONS...

SQUEEZE

SEE YOU LATER.

SORRY FOR BOTHERING YOU!

I'M GLAD NOTHING HAPPENED.

YEAH.

...

SORRY.
I'M SORRY.
HM?
HUH?
BUT WHY?
WHY?
BECAUSE...
...
I'LL GO FIRST THEN.
I'M SORRY I REACTED SO BADLY.
YOU'RE THE FIRST PERSON I'VE BEEN IN LOVE WITH.
BUT IT'S ONLY NATURAL THAT YOU'VE BEEN IN LOVE BEFORE.

I MUST'VE BEEN HARD TO BE AROUND.
I'M SORRY.
YAMATO...
I LOVE YOU.
YEAH, I KNOW...
I DECIDED THAT I WOULDN'T SAVE ANY GIRLS BUT YOU...
...BUT I ENDED UP SAVING HER ANYWAY.
I REALLY CAN'T FIND THE RIGHT WORDS.
I'M SORRY...
I'M PATHETIC.

NO, THAT'S A GOOD THING, TAKEO!
ONE OF THE THINGS I LOVE ABOUT YOU IS HOW YOU HELP EVERYONE.
WORRYING ABOUT WHETHER A GIRL YOU SAVE WILL FALL IN LOVE WITH YOU IS *MY* PROBLEM.
AND SO IS FEELING UNCOM-FORTABLE WHEN YOU TALK TO OTHER GIRLS.
BUT...
HERE'S THE THING...
I MADE UP MY MIND!
EVEN IF...
...ANOTHER GIRL FELL IN LOVE WITH YOU...
I WON'T LET ANY OF THAT GET ME DOWN ANYMORE.

...I WON'T LOSE TO HER. I'D FIGHT FOR YOU!
I WON'T LET ANYONE ELSE HAVE YOU.
SO YOU STAY JUST THE WAY YOU ARE.

YOU CAN BE THERE FOR EVERY-ONE.
YAMATO-!
BUT...
...I'D LIKE IT...
...IF THERE WERE A FEW MINUTES EVERY DAY...
...WHEN YOU ONLY BELONG TO ME.

I REALLY LOVE YOU.
THAT WOULD BE ENOUGH TO MAKE ME HAPPY.
STARTING RIGHT THIS MOMENT...
...I BELONG ONLY TO YOU!

I'LL BE RIGHT HERE UNTIL SOMEONE IS IN TROUBLE.
OKAY!
YAMATO...
APRIL 13TH AND SEPTEMBER 13TH ARE DAYS WE CELEBRATE!
I REMEMBERED.
WOW!
BUT THERE ARE MORE DAYS THAN THAT.
I DON'T THINK YOU CAN REMEMBER THEM ALL.
MAKE A CHART FOR ME.
OKAY.
THANK YOU.
LET'S BE HAPPY FOREVER.

Hello, this is Kawahara! (The writer.)

In 2012, many people supported Takeo and his friends. It was a year full of great memories. Thank you so much.

Once I send in my storyboard, I can't wait to see what Aruko will draw. I laugh and cry along with the rest of you! Aruko, thank you for drawing such cute characters!

This is volume 3! I'm so happy! Thank you very much!

Sunakawa is really cool. He's especially cool in the last chapter!

← Small face

I hope you'll keep supporting us and pick up volume 4. Kawahara out!

Aruko! Takeo is really difficult!

His eyes look dead.

The first time around, I skim through it, but the second time around, I read through it slowly. The background characters make funny faces! Takeo has strange reactions or clothes! Sunakawa acts like a Buddha...! It's all hilarious and gets more interesting the more I consume it. Kinda like how I feel about dried squid.

I hope you read this manga over and over again.

Aruko came up with 99 percent of the idea for Takeo's dad. I love it. Just looking at his face makes me laugh. It's so amusing just to see him there. I wonder what it is that I find so funny about him?

(*To show how little I do)

I drew out a storyboard. Aruko takes something like this and turns it into a comic.

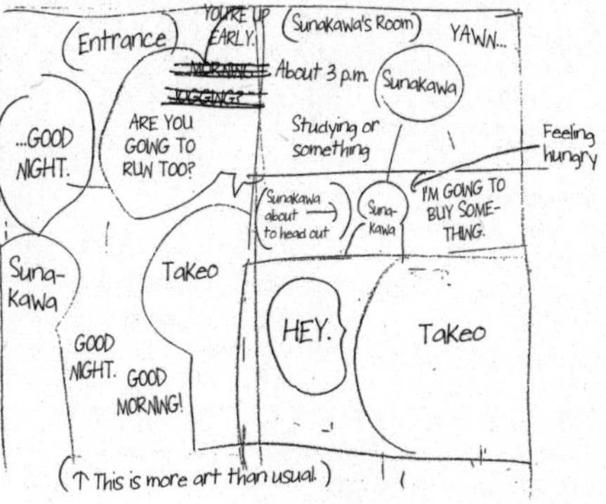

When Aruko turns this into manga, it's like magic!

MY

SHUEI HIGH SCHO

1-6

GOOD LUCK AT THE SPORTS TOURNAMENT!

OCTOBER 4

DAY DUTY

RAH!

RAH!

YEAH!

ALL RIGHT, GROUP 3!

C'MON!

THE GOAL'S RIGHT IN FRONT OF YOU! IT'S WIDE OPEN!

GOOOOO!

GODA!!
CATCH
AW, MAN! HAVING TAKEO AS GOALIE ISN'T FAIR!
GIVE US A BREAK, GROUP 6!
!!
WE CAN BARELY SEE THE GOAL!
LOB!!
HE THROWS THE BALL LIKE A BULLET!
HE MOVES WAY TOO FAST TO SEE!
FWIP
FWIP
FWIP

YOU'RE PLAYING THE FINAL GAME? THAT'S AMAZING!
YOU'RE UP AGAINST THIRD-YEARS NEXT, RIGHT? GOOD LUCK!
THANKS.
YOU'RE OUR GOOD-LUCK CHARM, MAN!
TAKEO'S THE AMAZING ONE, THOUGH.
LET'S DO THIS!
GODA!!
BUT NO PRESSURE, FACING *THAT* GOALIE...
HE ONLY *LOOKS* THAT CLOSE.
BET WE DON'T SCORE AT ALL.
OUR WINNERS ARE...
...FIRST-YEARS, GROUP 6!
CONGRATULATIONS!
WE DID IT!
YEAH!
THEY BROKE OUR SPIRIT...
USING TAKEO ISN'T FAIR...
THIRD-YEARS

WE DID IT, TAKEO!

GODA!!

...

THE BOYS WERE WONDERFUL!

CONGRATULATIONS!

"CONGRATULATIONS, TAKEO!"

I WONDER...

...WHAT YAMATO'S UP TO RIGHT NOW.
I HOPE SHE'S HAVING A GOOD DAY.
DING!
LOCKER ROOM

AH!

✉ From Yamato

How're you doing, Takeo?✧
I'm doing great!
I'm going skating with everyone today!
If you're free, would you like to come with some friends??
We'll be at the Shisuta Town Skating Rink.
This month, students can get in for just 300 yen!

SHE'S DOING GREAT.
I'M DOING GREAT TOO, YAMATO!
WHO WANTS TO GO SKATING WITH YAMATO AND HER FRIENDS AFTER THIS?
WOOHOO!
YOUR GIRLFRIEND?! AND HER FRIENDS?!
YOU WENT LAST TIME.
I WANNA GO!
I'M GOING TOO!
I'VE GOT WORK, BUT I'LL CALL IN SICK.
IT'S MY TURN!
I DON'T LIKE BEING COLD.
GRAB
YOU'LL BE WARM IF YOU MOVE AROUND.
I'VE NEVER SKATED BEFORE.
NEITHER HAVE I.
Re:
I'm free.
I'm bringing five friends.
Is that all right?
Absolutely!
How lucky!
It's the perfect number.
I've got five friends with me too!
LUCKY, HUH?
LOOKS LIKE IT...

TAKEO!
SORRY TO KEEP YOU WAITING!
IT'S OKAY. WE WEREN'T WAITING LONG.
SORRY!
I HAD TO RETAKE A KANJI TEST.
DO YOU HAVE TROUBLE WITH KANJI?
NOPE! I'M GOOD AT THEM.
BUT HALFWAY THROUGH, I MISSED A QUESTION ...
...SO MY ANSWERS WERE ALL OFF BY ONE.
DIDN'T YOU HAVE A LEFTOVER ANSWER SPACE?
YEAH, BUT I THOUGHT IT WAS JUST EXTRA.
HOW'VE YOU BEEN?
GOOD!
YOU WEREN'T STRESSED, WERE YOU?
HEH HEH...
HEE HEE...
NOT REALLY, NO.
...

RINKO'S A GREAT STUDENT.
YEAH, SHE'S VERY FOCUSED.
SHE GETS SOME OF THE BEST GRADES AT SCHOOL.
SUNA'S A GOOD STUDENT TOO.
REALLY?
EEEE! I FIGURED!
CUT IT OUT. I'M AVERAGE.
WHAT ABOUT YOU, TAKEO?
I'M BELOW AVERAGE.
HA HA...
I SEE.
BELOW AVERAGE, HUH?

I GUESS IT'S MORE LIKE I'M RIGHT NEAR THE BOTTOM...
SWOOSH
WAIT UP, TAKEO!
HOLD ON TO ME.
OKAY.
WHOA ...!
SLIP
SLIP
TAKE IT SLOW.
ISN'T THIS YOUR FIRST TIME SKATING, TAKEO?
HOW ARE YOU SO GOOD?
JUST KEEP MOVING ONE FOOT AFTER THE OTHER.
...
HUH?
HEY...
MURMUR
INCREDIBLE!
WHO *IS* THAT GUY?!

A TRIPLE AXEL...
...INTO...
...A LAYBACK INA BAUER ...!
...
IT'S LIKE WATCHING HUMAN EVOLUTION IN FAST-FORWARD...
COCOA

I'M GONNA GET A DRINK.
NOW I'M OVER-HEATING.
MY LEGS ARE FROZEN.
SCRATCH
SCRATCH
WHAT'S WRONG?
OH— COMING INTO A WARM ROOM AFTER BEING COLD...
...MADE MY THIGH ITCHY. IT'S THE INCREASED BLOOD FLOW!
I LOVE THIS GIRL.
DIDN'T SOMEONE GIVE YOU A BUSINESS CARD EARLIER?
OH, THAT'S RIGHT. SOMEONE TRIED TO SCOUT TAKEO.
HMM?
I SEE...
YEAH, I CAN SEE WHY!
HE'S BRILLIANT AT SKATING.
THAT THING EARLIER WAS A COINCIDENCE. I WAS TRYING TO CATCH MY BALANCE.

TODAY...
...WE HAD A SPORTS TOURNAMENT.
TAKEO WAS OUR GOALIE, SO WE WON WITHOUT THE OTHER TEAM SCORING ANY POINTS!
THAT'S AMAZING!
HA HA HA! I CAN SEE THAT HAPPENING.
I WISH I'D SEEN IT!
YOU MUST'VE LOOKED SO COOL.
BASHFUL
ARE YOU GOOD AT ALL SPORTS, TAKEO?
HE'S AWFUL AT BASKET-BALL.
YEAH, THAT'S TRUE.
HE FALLS FOR EVERY FEINT.
PFFT
HE FALLS FOR THEM REALLY BADLY!
HA HA HA!

AND HE'S A TERRIBLE DANCER.
HE REALLY IS!
HIS STEPS ARE HUGE.
ACTUALLY, LAST TIME WE HAD GYM CLASS...
HA HA HA!
IT SOUNDS WONDERFUL.
I WISH WE WENT TO THE SAME SCHOOL.
HEE HEE...
THE SAME SCHOOL?
HUH...
SEE YOU!
BYE!

TAKEO, LOOK AT THE MOON!
IT'S SO FULL.
IT'S STILL LIGHT OUT TOO.
ARE YOU PLANNING TO GO TO COLLEGE?
I DON'T KNOW. I HAVEN'T REALLY THOUGHT ABOUT IT.
WHAT ABOUT YOU?

"I'D LIKE TO GO TO THE SAME SCHOOL AS YOU."

"RINKO'S A GREAT STUDENT."
YAMATO, NO.
YOU DON'T NEED TO PICK A DIFFERENT SCHOOL.
HUH? BUT—
I JUST HAVE TO STUDY HARDER.
I'LL GET MY GRADES UP AS HIGH AS YOURS...
...AND THEN WE'LL GO TO THE COLLEGE YOU WANT.
TAKEO...
DON'T WORRY. JUST LEAVE IT TO ME.

I STILL HAVE TWO YEARS BEFORE ENTRANCE EXAMS! I'LL MANAGE!
ER...
YEAH!
STARTING NOW, I'LL STUDY EVERY SINGLE DAY!
"I'D LIKE TO GO TO THE SAME SCHOOL AS YOU..."
"I'D LIKE TO GO..."
"I'D LIKE TO..."
ALL RIGHT!
ABSOLUTE VICTORY
BOOM!
BADOOM!
WORLD HISTORY
...

BA
SUNA!
I HAVE A FAVOR TO ASK!
YOU'RE THE ONLY ONE WHO CAN HELP ME!
TWITCH
DOOOM
...
WHAT IS IT?
HELP ME GET ACCEPTED TO MURASAKI FUJI UNIVERSITY.
HUH?
I'M BEG-GING YOU!
I'D HELP WITH A NORMAL FAVOR...
...BUT IT'S IMPOSSIBLE FOR YOU TO GET IN THERE.
UGH
IMPOS-SIBLE, HUH?
BECAUSE I ONLY STUDY RIGHT BEFORE TESTS...
YOU NEVER DO MUCH STUDYING EVEN THEN.
BUT WHY THAT UNIVER-SITY?
IT'S WHERE YAMATO WANTS TO GO.
REALLY? I THOUGHT SHE'D BE A PASTRY CHEF.
BUT SHE SAID SHE'D RATHER GO TO THE SAME SCHOOL AS ME.
AH.

SHE WANTS US TO GO TO COLLEGE TOGETHER.
I WANT TO DO ALL I CAN TO MAKE THAT HAPPEN.
...OKAY, GOT IT.
WELL, WANT TO START WITH ENGLISH?
IT'S HANDY FOR LIBERAL ARTS AND SCIENCES.
THANKS, SUNA!
DON'T MENTION IT.
COUGH
LET'S TEST OUT YOUR BASIC VOCAB.
DEFINE "GET."
LUNGE
IT'S LIKE...
PULL
...THIS.
HOW ABOUT "FOR-GET"?
IT'S LIKE...
...THIS.
THAT'S...
...PRETTY ACCUR-ATE.
YES!
YEAH, THAT'S ACCURATE TOO.
HA HA...
OOOOH!

DING!

OH!

IT'S YAMATO.

Hi, Takeo!
You know, even if Murasaki Fuji is impossible, Aobeni University and Matsucha University are both nearby.
I want to apply to a liberal arts school.
There's a mock exam coming up soon.
I figure I don't need to take it yet, but if you want to take it, then I will too!
Want to try it together??

HOW ARE AOBENI OR MATSUCHA?

THEY'RE NOT EASY, BUT MORE REALISTIC THAN MURASAKI FUJI.

THAT'S DEFINITELY THE HARDEST.

I SEE.

A MOCK EXAM, HUH?

THAT'S A GOOD GOAL TO AIM FOR.

MURASAKI FUJI IT IS!

WELL, GIVE IT YOUR BEST SHOT.

OKAY!

YOU'RE TOO LOUD...

HUH?!
IS TAKEO STUDYING?!
WHAT IS THIS? WHAT'S GOING ON? LET'S PLAY!
SHH!
SUNA...
THIS IS BAD. I CAN'T FACE MY OPPONENT.
NEMESIS: MOCK EXAM
I CAN'T THROW IT OR WRESTLE IT...
CONFOUNDED
THERE'S A WAY TO FIGURE IT OUT.
YOU NEED TO HAVE SOME MATCHES!
THUD
COLLECTION of PROBLEMS
HOW MANY BATTLES AM I FIGHTING?!

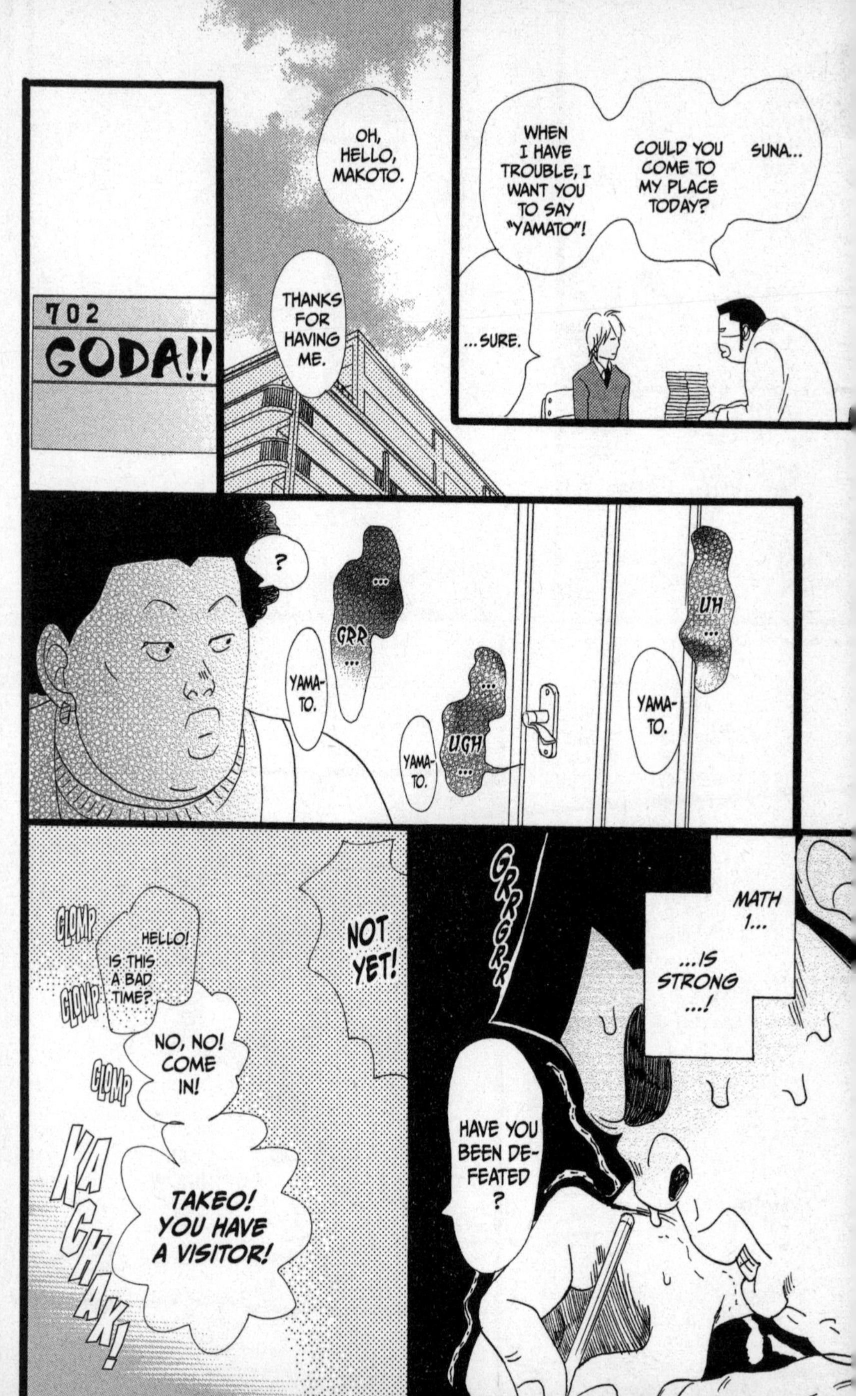
SUNA...
COULD YOU COME TO MY PLACE TODAY?
WHEN I HAVE TROUBLE, I WANT YOU TO SAY "YAMATO"!
...SURE.
OH, HELLO, MAKOTO.
THANKS FOR HAVING ME.
702
GODA!!
UH...
YAMA-TO.
UGH...
YAMA-TO.
GRR...
YAMA-TO.
?
GRRGRR
MATH 1...
...IS STRONG...!
HAVE YOU BEEN DE-FEATED?
NOT YET!
CLOMP
HELLO! IS THIS A BAD TIME?
CLOMP
NO, NO! COME IN!
CLOMP
TAKEO! YOU HAVE A VISITOR!
KACHAK!

YAMATO!
HI!
STARE
YOU TEXTED AND SAID YOU'RE STUDYING?
BRAINS WORK BETTER WITH SUGAR, SO I MADE SOME CHOCOLATES.
OH, BUT I DIDN'T MAKE THEM FROM CACAO. I MADE CHOCOLATES, BUT I DIDN'T MAKE CHOCOLATE...
HUH? WHAT AM I SAYING?
STARE
POP
I'M GOING TO MAKE SOME TEA. MAKE YOURSELF COMFORTABLE!
TAKEO, GIVE ME A HAND?
OKAY.
OH!
THANK YOU!
TAKEO...
IS THAT GIRL YOUR GIRLFRIEND?
YEAH, SHE IS.

THIS TEA WON'T DO AT ALL.
SLAM
I'M GOING TO GET SOME BETTER TEA.
TOSS
DO YOU NEED MY HELP?
ZOOM
NO, I DON'T. GO TO YOUR ROOM.
WAIT THERE.
WHERE'S YOUR MOM?
SHE WENT TO BUY SOME TEA.
WHAT? SHE WENT TO THAT MUCH TROUBLE ?!
I FEEL KIND OF BAD...
ISN'T SHE PREGNANT? SHE SEEMS AWFULLY ENERGETIC.
I TOLD HER YOU'RE MY GIRLFRIEND.
HUH? OH, OKAY.
SHOULD I NOT HAVE TOLD HER?
I'M SORRY FOR INTERFERING. I WASN'T PLANNING ON STAYING.
I GOT NERVOUS TALKING TO YOUR MOM.

NO.
I'M GLAD.
YAY.
OH, YOU HAVE THE SAME WORLD HISTORY TEXTBOOK AS ME!
AND THE SAME MATH BOOK TOO.
SO WE CAN DISCUSS THEM!
THE QUESTIONS I HAVE TO MEMORIZE, I'LL DO ON MY OWN.
doskoi
STUDYING IS SURPRISINGLY FUN.
SLAM

DO YOU LIKE TEA, MISS YAMATO?
HERE YOU GO.
OH, YES. I LOVE IT. THANK YOU VERY MUCH!
I'VE NEVER SEEN THOSE CUPS BEFORE. WHERE'D SHE GET THEM?
DID SHE JUST BUY THEM?
MAKE YOURSELF AT HOME, OKAY?
OKAY!
BUT I HAVEN'T CALLED MY PARENTS.
I'LL HEAD HOME AFTER TEA.
THAT'S A SHAME.
TAKEO, DEAR, WALK HER HOME.
OKAY.
DON'T OVERDO IT, TAKEO.
AFTER HEARING EVERYONE TALK ABOUT YOU, I THOUGHT IT'D BE NICE TO GO TO THE SAME SCHOOL...
...BUT IT'S NOT THE MOST IMPORTANT THING.
doskoi
WE SHOULD HAVE FUN EVEN IF WE GO TO DIFFERENT SCHOOLS.

GOING TO THE SAME COLLEGE AS YAMATO WOULD BE GREAT.
I THOUGHT THE SAME THING THOUGH.
IT'D BE REALLY NICE.
YEAH! BEING TOGETHER IS THE MOST FUN. DO YOUR BEST, TAKEO!
OKAY!
AND I WILL TOO. WE'LL BOTH DO OUR BEST!
I'M GOING TO BE STUDYING ON THE WEEKEND TOO, SO COME OVER IF YOU HAVE SOME FREE TIME.
HANG OUT WITH ME.
ALL RIGHT! I'LL COME OVER TOMORROW!
LET'S STUDY TOGETHER.
I THOUGHT ABOUT HOW NICE IT'D BE...
...IF YAMATO WAS ALWAYS RIGHT BESIDE ME.

YAMATO'S COMING OVER TO-MORROW.
YAMATO?
THAT'S *MISS* YAMATO.
SHE'S TAKEO'S GIRL-FRIEND.
GIRL-FRIEND?
WHAT'S SHE LIKE?
SHE SEEMS VERY NICE.
GOOD FOR YOU.
THANKS.
Z Z Z Z
CLANK
PLUNK
SPLISH
SPLISH
SPLISH

SPLISH SPLISH
SPLISH
EXTRA TOUGH RICE CRACKERS
WHAT ARE YOU DOING?
DID I WAKE YOU?
I HAPPENED TO BE UP.
GO BACK TO BED.
WIPE
WIPE
...
...

I'M GOING TO LAY OUT NEW TOWELS IN THE BATHROOM.
I'M PUTTING OUT NEW SLIPPERS.
MOM AND DAD...
...DRESSED UP A LITTLE.

DING DONG
WELCOME!
MAKE YOURSELF AT HOME!
OH, HELLO! I HOPE I'M NOT INTRUDING.

HUH? YOUR ROOM LOOKS DIFFERENT.
IT'S BECAUSE YOU WERE COMING OVER.
MY MOM CLEANED IT.
WHAT?! I FEEL KIND OF BAD.
BUT KINDA HAPPY TOO.
SIT ANYWHERE YOU LIKE.
OKAY.
OKAY! SHALL WE START STUDYING?
YEAH. I'LL DO MY OWN WORK!
WE'LL FOCUS HARD AND NOT TALK FOR 30 MINUTES.
OKAY, STARTING NOW.
READY?
GO!
KNOCK KNOCK!

TAKEO, DO YOU HAVE A MOMENT?
KA-CHAK!
I HAVEN'T INTRODUCED MYSELF.
I'M TAKEO'S FATHER.
OH! YES! PLEASED TO MEET YOU. I'M RINKO YAMATO!
I HEAR YOU'RE TAKING GOOD CARE OF TAKEO.
YES! I MEAN, HE'S TAKING GOOD CARE OF ME TOO!
LOOK AFTER TAKEO.
I WILL!
I'LL LEAVE YOU KIDS ALONE.
SHUT

I WAS SO NERVOUS!
I THOUGHT YOU TOOK AFTER YOUR MOM, BUT YOU TAKE AFTER YOUR DAD TOO!
YOU THINK SO?
OKAY, THEN— 30 MINUTES, STARTING NOW!
OKAY.
SLAM
ARE YOU HUNGRY?
DO YOU LIKE RICE CRACKERS?
YES! AND I BROUGHT SWEET SNACKS TODAY. I'M GLAD WE GOT DIFFERENT THINGS.
OH MY, DID YOU MAKE THESE? THAT'S AMAZING.
OOH, THEY'RE SCRUMPTIOUS.
HOW LONG HAVE YOU BEEN DATING TAKEO?

WE'RE TRYING TO STUDY! OUT!
SLAM!
WHAT'S HIS PROB-LEM?
PHEW...
KNOCK KNOCK
KA-CHAK
DO YOU FOLLOW GOLF, YOUNG LADY?
UM... GOLF? I DON'T WATCH IT VERY OFTEN.
IT'S FUN. DO YOU KNOW ISHIKAWA?
YES, I DO.
MY DAD WATCHES AT HOME.
YOUR DAD IS A GOLFER? I'M A GOLFER TOO.
WE CAN'T GET ANYTHING DONE HERE!

SURE.
701
SUNAKAWA
MY PARENTS AREN'T HOME TODAY, SO WHATEVER'S FINE.
I WAS STUDYING TOO.
YOUR PLACE IS ALWAYS CLEAN.
SORRY FOR THE INTRUSION.
TAKEO, I'LL ASK YOU SOME QUESTIONS.
OKAY.
WHEN DID WORLD WAR II START?
1939!
AWESOME! THAT'S CORRECT! ♡
ASK SOMETHING A LITTLE HARDER.
HMM, LET'S SEE...
...I DON'T GET IT.
Modern Literature Selections

I DON'T UNDERSTAND WHY THIS GUY IS GOING BACK AND FORTH BETWEEN TWO WOMEN.
TAKEO, THE TEST ISN'T GOING TO ASK FOR YOUR OPINION.
JUST ANSWER THE QUESTION.
HE'S BEING SO DIS-RESPECTFUL TO THEM!
I THINK SO TOO.
HE SHOULD KNOW WHO HE LIKES.
...
YOU TOO, YAMATO?
TAKEO, WOULDN'T YOU FIND IT HARD TO DECIDE IF THERE WERE TWO OF YAMATO?
AND YAMATO, WOULDN'T YOU BE UNABLE TO DECIDE IF THERE WERE TWO OF TAKEO?
!

!!
YAMATO...
TAKEO...
YAMATO...
TAKEO ...
WHICH OF YOU IS REAL?!
ME!
I'M THE REAL ONE! WHAT ABOUT YOU, TAKEO?!
ME!
I'M TAKEO!
THAT'D BE HORRIBLE! I WOULDN'T KNOW WHO TO PICK!
NOOOO!
I DON'T KNOW!
THIS ISN'T WHAT I THOUGHT WOULD HAPPEN, BUT WHATEVER.
MOVING RIGHT ALONG.
THUD!!
TAKEO ?!

OH!
ZZZ...
ZZZ...
HE'S ASLEEP...
HE'S BEEN STUDYING HARD.
I'VE NEVER SEEN HIM STUDY LIKE THIS.
Byzantium
Carolingian Dynasty
Second Frankish Dynasty
Carolingian
TAKEO...
LET'S LET HIM SLEEP FOR HALF AN HOUR OR SO.
I'M GOING TO MAKE SOME TEA.
SHUT

...
TAKEO, I THINK IT'D BE GREAT IF WE COULD GO TO THE SAME SCHOOL.
BUT EVEN IF WE CAN'T, I WANT TO ALWAYS BE WITH YOU.
...
ROLL
CHAK
DO YOU WANT COFFEE OR ROASTED TEA?

KRII
SHUT
EEEEK! WAIT A SECOND, SUNAKAWA!
NO, NO. CARRY ON.
IT'S NOT WHAT YOU THINK!
I DIDN'T SEE ANYTHING.
DON'T TELL TAKEO!
DON'T TELL TAKEO I DID THINGS TO HIM WHILE HE WAS SLEEPING!
DID THINGS?
I WON'T.
OH!
OH, NO! I FELL ASLEEP.
HEY, HE WOKE UP.
TH-THMP

WELL, GOOD LUCK.
THANKS FOR LETTING US COME OVER, SUNAKAWA.
IT'S STILL LIGHT, SO I CAN GO HOME BY MYSELF.
OKAY! SEE YOU!
...
SCORING
SUNA, ARE YOU GOING TO COLLEGE?
YEAH, I GUESS SO.
I HAVEN'T DECIDED WHERE YET, THOUGH.
OH, YEAH?
I HAVEN'T THOUGHT AT ALL ABOUT WHAT I'M GOING TO DO.
WANT TO GO TO THE SAME COLLEGE?
WHY DO YOU ASK?
IT'D BE FUN TO HAVE YOU AROUND.
WELL...
I'M NOT GONNA AIM LOW, SO YOU NEED TO KEEP STUDYING HARD.
OH.
GOT IT!

THE POINT OF STUDYING IS TO LEARN THINGS THAT'LL HELP YOU AVOID MAKING THE WRONG CHOICES IN LIFE.
SO YOU PROBABLY DON'T NEED IT.
WHY?
EXACTLY.
YOU DON'T NEED TO UNDER-STAND.
?
HEH...
YOU KNOW, I CAN ALMOST SEE YOU GETTING INTO MURASAKI FUJI.
REALLY?
I DON'T UNDER-STAND COMPLEX THINGS.
AND I'M...

...NOT REALLY GOOD AT STUDYING.
BUT IF I CAN MAKE THEM HAPPY...
...I'LL TRY TO OVERCOME MY LIMITATIONS.

MOCK EXAM ROOM

TAKEO...

DON'T TALK TO ME. EVERYTHING I MEMORIZED IS TRYING TO SPILL OUT OF MY HEAD.
LOOK OUT—
gambler
CRASH
TEN THINGS JUST SPILLED OUT!
HELP ME PICK THEM UP!
HEY, YAMATO.
YAMATO!
CALM DOWN, TAKEO!
OKAY!
DO YOU HAVE YOUR PENCIL?
SWISH
HOW ABOUT YOUR ERASER?
SWISH
THEN I'LL SEE YOU AFTER!
OKAY!
DING!

YOU MAY BEGIN!
ALL RIGHT!
YOU'RE GOING DOWN!!
MARK-UP
HMM...
THIS QUESTION ...
I THINK THEY'LL ASK THIS.
AH, YAMATO HELPED ME WITH THIS ONE!
I MADE YOU
FLASH-CARDS!
I CAN TAKE DOWN WORLD HISTORY!
OKAY!
JUST A LITTLE ...
PRETTY GOOD...
I CAN DO THIS!
RAGH RAGH RAGH
GASP
QUESTION LIST
ANSWERS
...
CLATTER...

MY ANSWERS ARE...
...OFF BY ONE SOME-WHERE!!
"MY ANSWERS WERE ALL OFF BY ONE."
WHERE ?!
STARE
WHERE IS IT?!
WHERE DID I MAKE THE MISTAKE ?!
I CAN'T GIVE UP!
I'VE GOT TO FIX AS MANY AS POSSIBLE!
RUB RUB RUB
RIIIING
TIME'S UP!
PENCILS DOWN.

PANT
PANT
PANT
PANT
PANT
PANT
PANT
PANT
WHAT HAPPENED, TAKEO?!
YOU'RE DRENCHED !!
?!
HIS ANSWERS WERE OFF BY ONE QUESTION.
I FIXED AS MANY AS I COULD, BUT I DON'T KNOW IF IT HELPED.
THEY HELPED ME STUDY...
I SAID THAT I'D DO MY BEST...
AT LEAST IT WASN'T THE REAL EXAM.
THAT'S RIGHT!
THIS IS JUST THE BEGINNING!
I'M SO SORRY, YOU GUYS.
...
RIGHT.

THAT'S TRUE.

I'LL DEFEAT THE NEXT SUBJECT!

LET'S GO FOR IT!

I'LL HAVE MORE CHANCES.

Mock Exam Results

Shuei High School Takeo Goda

First Choice	Murasaki Fuji University	X Recommendation Impossible

...

WHAT'S AN "X RECOMMENDATION"?

IT'S AN "X" BESIDE "RECOMMENDATION."

IT MEANS THEY CAN'T RECOMMEND YOU.

"S" MEANS YOU PASSED WITH DISTINCTION. "A" MEANS YOU PASSED.

"IMPOSSIBLE" ...

SHOCK

I'M GOING TO CALL YAMATO.

...

I SEE. WELL, YOU COULDN'T ENROLL AT MURASAKI FUJI ANYWAY.
YEAH.
HA HA! SPEAKING OF IMPOSSIBLE, I DIDN'T DO VERY WELL EITHER.
LISTEN. IF WE WORK HARD, I THINK WE CAN GO TO HAKUTO UNIVERSITY.
SO LET'S AIM FOR THAT!
I'M GONNA DO MY BEST.
YAMATO ...
SO YOU'RE GIVING UP ON MURASAKI FUJI?
HA HA! I'M FINE WITH THAT.
BECAUSE YOU WOULDN'T BE ABLE TO GO.
I MEAN, MURASAKI FUJI IS A WOMEN'S COLLEGE.

IT... IT'S WHAT?!

YEAH. IT WAS NICE TO THINK THAT YOU'D BE THERE...

...BUT IT REALLY WAS IMPOSSIBLE.

HEH

YOU TRICKED ME, SUNA!

HUH? SUNAKAWA?

TO BE CONTINUED...

BONUS MANGA

TAKEO, AGE 5

LET'S GO TO THE PARK!

...SURE.

YAHOO!

TAKEO, AGE 10

WHY DO I KEEP FALLING INTO THIS HOLE?

PROBABLY BECAUSE YOU'RE NOT JUMPING.

DS

ABOUT TAKEO...
SUNA-KAWA'S OLDER SISTER (MIDDLE SCHOOL)
HE STICKS HIS FACE REALLY CLOSE TO THE SCREEN.
EVERY TIME.
DING DONG
MONITOR
BRIGHTNESS
SPEAKER
...
YOU'RE TOO CLOSE.
OH, RIGHT.
PFFFT
WHAT'S WRONG? DID SOMETHING FUNNY HAPPEN?
HA HA HA!
IT'S NOTHING.
LET'S GET TO SCHOOL!
...

NOW
I'M GOING TO THE BATH-ROOM!
...
SOMETIMES TAKEO PUTS HIS FACE REALLY CLOSE TO MINE.
I DON'T KNOW WHAT TO DO!
MY HEART STARTS RACING ...
YEAH.
I DON'T KNOW WHAT TO DO, EITHER.
IT'S HILARI-OUS.
HA HA HA!
HMM?
(CAME BACK)
WHAT'S GOING ON?
HANG IN THERE.
EEEE!
TH-THMP TH-THMP

THE END

When I drew the sketch for the one-shot, I wasn't thinking about what would happen later on. Some of my favorite characters, like Takeo's dad, didn't appear then, so I'm really glad it didn't just end there. Aruko and everyone else, thank you for your support.

– Kazune Kawahara

ARUKO is from Ishikawa Prefecture in Japan and was born on July 26 (a Leo!). She made her manga debut with *Ame Nochi Hare* (Clear After the Rain). Her other works include *Yasuko to Kenji*, and her hobbies include laughing and getting lost.

KAZUNE KAWAHARA is from Hokkaido Prefecture in Japan and was born on March 11 (a Pisces!). She made her manga debut at age 18 with *Kare no Ichiban Sukina Hito* (His Most Favorite Person). Her best-selling shojo manga series *High School Debut* is available in North America from VIZ Media. Her hobby is interior redecorating.

It's volume 3! In the beginning, I didn't think I'd get to draw this much. It's so fun and exciting every time I work on this series. I feel like I've been saved by Takeo and his friends many times now. I'm really glad to be a part of this. Thanks for reading!

– Aruko

MY LOVE STORY!!

Volume 3
Shojo Beat Edition

Story **KAZUNE KAWAHARA**
Art by **ARUKO**

English Adaptation ♡ **Ysabet Reinhardt MacFarlane**
Translation ♡ **JN Productions**
Touch-up Art & Lettering ♡ **Mark McMurray**
Design ♡ **Fawn Lau**
Editor ♡ **Amy Yu**

Printed in the U.S.A.

Published by VIZ Media, LLC
P.O. Box 77010
San Francisco, CA 94107

10 9 8 7 6 5 4 3 2 1
First printing, January 2015

You may be reading the **wrong way!!**

IT'S TRUE: In keeping with the original Japanese comic format, this book reads from right to left—so action, sound effects, and word balloons are completely reversed. This preserves the orientation of the original artwork—plus, it's fun! Check out the diagram shown here to get the hang of things, and then turn to the other side of the book to get started!

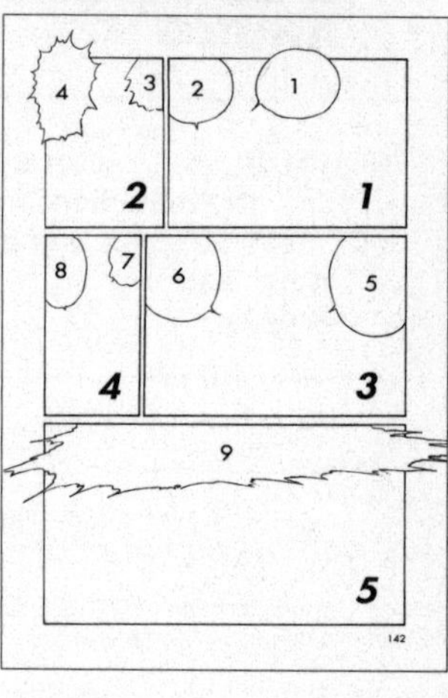